100 facts

SPIES

100 facts

SPIES

John Farndon

Consultant: Brian Williams

Miles
Kelly

First published in 2009 by Miles Kelly Publishing Ltd
Harding's Barn, Bardfield End Green, Thaxted, Essex, CM6 3PX

Copyright © Miles Kelly Publishing Ltd 2009

This edition published 2016

6 8 10 9 7

Publishing Director: Belinda Gallagher
Creative Director: Jo Cowan
Managing Editor: Rosie Neave
Editorial Assistant: Claire Philip
Volume Designers: Sally Lace, Simon Lee
Image Manager: Lorraine King
Indexer: Jane Parker
Production: Elizabeth Collins, Caroline Kelly
Reprographics: Stephan Davis, Jennifer Cozens, Thom Allaway, Anthony Cambray
Assets: Lorraine King

ISBN 978-1-78617-302-7

Printed in China

British Library Cataloguing-in-Publication Data
A catalogue record for this book is available from the British Library

ACKNOWLEDGEMENTS
The publishers would like to thank the following artists
who have contributed to this book:
Julian Baker, Mike Foster
All other artworks from the Miles Kelly Artwork Bank

The publishers would like to thank the following sources for the use of their photographs:
Cover: Blend Images/Alamy Stock Photo
Page 6–7 Reuters/Corbis; 8–9 Uriel Sinai/Pool/Reuters/Corbis; 9(r) Sipa Press/Rex Features;
10(bl) Photos 12/Alamy, (tr) Peter Horree/Alamy; 11(br) Bettmann/Corbis; 12(bl) Sipa Press/Rex Features,
(br) Pictorial Press Ltd/Alamy; 14–15 Getty Images, 14(bl) Corbis, 15(tl) Bettmann/Corbis; 16(tl) Brooks Kraft/Corbis,
(tc) Roger Ressmeyer/Corbis, (bl) Mikhail Klimentyev/Pool/epa/Corbis, (br) Dmitry Ersler/Fotolia; 17(t) Sipa Press/Rex Features,
(bl) Popperfoto/Getty Images; 18 (in screen) Alessandro Abbonizio/AFP/Getty Images, (screen) Ozphoto/Fotolia, (bc) Bettman/Corbis;
19(tl) David Heerde/Rex Features, (b) Greg Smith/Corbis; 20–21 Moviestorecollection.com, 21(tr) Cezaro de Luca/epa/Corbis;
22(tr) GustoImages/Science Photo Library; 23(t) Viktor Gmyria/Fotolia; 24 Ed Pritchard/Getty Images; 25(tr) Tek Image/Science Photo
Library, (b) Christopher Furlong/Getty Images; 26–27 Rex Features; 30(br) Bettmann/Corbis; 31(tl) Roman Ivaschenko/Fotolia;
32–33(bg) ktsdesign/Fotolia, 33(tr) Rex Features, (bl) Brooks Kraft/Corbis; 35 Moviestorecollection.com; 36(b) Sipa Press/Rex Features;
37(t) MGM/Pictorialpress.com, (br) Colin Anderson/Brand X/Corbis; 38(t) Corbis, 38–39 Joeygil/Dreamstime; 39(t) Corbis;
40 Reuters/Corbis; 41(br) NASA/Science Photo Library; 42 The Sun/Rex Features; 43(t) Rex Features, (b) Sutton-Hibbert/Rex Features;
44(b) Sean Gladwell/Fotolia; 45 Andrew Brookes, National Physical Laboratory/ Science Photo Library; 46 MGM/Everett/Rex Features;
47(tl) Miramax/Everett/Rex Features, (b) MGM/Everett/Rex Features

All other photographs are from:
Corel, digitalSTOCK, digitalvision, iStockphoto.com, John Foxx, PhotoAlto,
PhotoDisc, PhotoEssentials, PhotoPro, Stockbyte

Made with paper from a sustainable forest
www.mileskelly.net

Contents

What is a spy?

1 **Spies have to get important information from people without them knowing.** To do this they may have to pretend they're on the side of an enemy, or gain entry to secret places. The information they gather is called 'intelligence', so spies are known as intelligence officers or agents. The word espionage comes from the French word for spying, *espionnage*.

▼ Night-vision technology enables spies to observe targets under the cover of darkness. Night-vision binoculars have a range of over 200 metres even when it is totally dark.

The reasons for spying

2 **Many spies work for national governments.** Most nations employ spies to find out other nation's secrets. Spies gather information on enemy countries, as well as countries that may become hostile in the future. For example, during the 1950s and 60s, the US government sent spies to find out the Soviet Union government's secrets, and vice versa.

3 **Some spies try to find out about an enemy nation's secret battle plans and weapons.** This is probably the oldest form of spying. If you know what your enemy's plans are, you can work out how to defend yourself – or catch them by surprise. For this reason, military secrets are the most closely guarded of all.

Agents exchange top secret information.

4 Government spies may try to gather information on people who deal in illegal drugs. The illegal drugs trade makes, distributes and sells addictive drugs. Major drug dealers are powerful criminals who are hard to catch, so governments send spies into the illegal drugs trade to find out who the heads of drug rings really are, and gather enough evidence against them to send them to prison.

▼ In 1999, narcotics agents discovered suitcases of illegal drugs worth £7.6 million in an apartment in France, which had been smuggled into the country using a private plane. Police need inside information to pick up big hauls of drugs, which can mean sending spies into drug dealers' networks.

▲ An explosion rocks the desert during a military training exercise. Intelligence agencies target countries or groups of people that have or are suspected of having WMDs (weapons of mass destruction) to find out if they pose a threat.

5 Terrorist groups are important targets for spies. Governments need to find out about possible terrorist attacks before they happen. This can be achieved by sending spies 'undercover' to join terrorist groups. The spies try to find out information about the terrorists and what they are planning.

Spying in the past

6 **The first spy service was called the King's Eye.** Around 2700 years ago, the Assyrian king Sargon II ruled an empire in the Middle East and used spies to seek out any trouble. Citizens who criticized the king were severely punished. One order given was: "If there is a ditch in the countryside or the city, make this man disappear."

▶ A winged lion from the palace of King Sargon II, who set up the world's first government spy network.

Dowbleth σ
where as of the from
𐤐 𐤌 𐤌𐤚 𐤗
in wich is what say me m
𐤗 𐤂 𐤇 𐤌 𐤍 𐤌
I pray you Mte your n

▲▼ Above: A sample of a code that Walsingham's spies intercepted and deciphered. Below: A scene from the 1998 movie *Elizabeth*.

Walsingham

Elizabeth I

7 **Sir Francis Walsingham, spymaster of Elizabeth I, trapped a queen.** In the 1500s, Walsingham set up a spy network to protect Elizabeth from Catholic plots. Aided by his ace code-cracker Thomas Phellipes, Walsingham set up a brilliant 'sting' operation to catch Mary Queen of Scots sending coded messages plotting to kill Elizabeth. Mary was tried and beheaded.

I DON'T BELIEVE IT!

In the 5th century BC, the Greek general Histaeus had battle plans tattooed onto a slave's shaven head. After the hair grew back again the slave travelled safely to Histaeus' allies, who shaved his head to read the message.

A sample of the code used by the Culper Spy Ring during the American War of Independence (1775–1783).

USE OF	MEANS
e	a
f	b
g	c
h	d
i	e
j	f
a	g
b	h
c	i
d	j
o	k
m	l
n	m

USE OF	MEANS
711	General Washington
712	Clinton
713	Tryon
721	Major Tallmadge alias John Bolton
722	Abraham Woodhull alias Samuel Culper
723	Robert Townsend alias Samuel Culper, Jr.
724	Austin Roe

USE OF	MEANS
15	advice
28	appointment
60	better
121	day
156	deliver
151	disorder
178	enemy
174	express
230	guineas
286	ink
309	infantry
317	importance
322	inquiry

8

Cardinal Richelieu was one of the most famous spymasters. Richelieu worked for King Louis XIII of France in the 17th century. He set up a 'Cabinet Noir' (Black Chamber) to intercept letters and steal secrets for the king. He had a network of spies across Europe, some of whom worked undercover as dancing and fencing teachers.

9

Harriet Tubman was a slave who became a spy. Brought up as a slave in southern USA, Harriet escaped to the north in 1849. For years she ran the Underground Railroad – an escape route for slaves. During the US Civil War (1861–1865), Harriet became one of the north's key spies against southern slave-owners, making 19 rescue missions and freeing hundreds of slaves.

Over the course of ten years and at great personal risk, Harriet Tubman (left) helped to free hundreds of slaves, some of whom are shown with her here.

10

America's first spy network was set up by George Washington. During the American War of Independence (1775–1783) Washington set up a clever spy network called the Culper Spy Ring. The Culper spies sent messages about the movements of the British forces in secret ink called Jay's Sympathetic Stain. They also sent messages by hanging out different clothes on washing lines.

World at war

11 In World War I (1914–1918), beautiful Dutch dancer Mata Hari spied for Germany *and* France. She used her beauty to gain men's trust and get information. To the Germans she was agent H-21, but she was also spying for France. The French discovered that she was spying for Germany when they intercepted a coded message, and she was executed.

◀ France became aware of Mata Hari's dealings with Germany in 1917. She was arrested and tried by a military court, which sentenced her to death.

Despite being shot in the leg and the eye, Cher Ami delivered the US soldiers' message.

13 A pigeon saved the day in World War I! At Verdun, France, a group of American soldiers became surrounded by German troops. Other American forces began bombing the Germans, unaware that they were also bombing their own men. The surrounded Americans sent out Cher Ami the pigeon with a message to stop the bombing. Cher Ami got the message through, and was awarded the *Croix de Guerre*, the highest French medal.

12 The SOE (Special Operations Executive) was a British spy network in World War II (1939–1945). They worked to sabotage the Germans and support French resistance fighters. A famous SOE spy was Violette Szabo, a young woman who was skilled with a rifle. She was captured by the Germans and killed during her second mission in 1944.

▶ Szabo began working for the SOE after her husband, Etienne, was killed fighting for Britain in North Africa. This photo was taken around the time of their marriage.

Lightbulbs

Spare cables

Rotors spin to encrypt each letter typed on the keys

Messages were typed using the keys

Cables plugged into the plugboard encrypted the message further

14 During World War II, the German navy sent messages in a code created by a machine called Enigma. German submarines called U-boats sank British and American ships across the Atlantic. The British intercepted the messages to the U-boats, but could not understand them. Brilliant code-breakers in British intelligence at Bletchley Park (also known as Station X), Buckinghamshire, UK, worked to crack the code, and built the world's first successful computer to help them. They succeeded in breaking the code, and many ships were saved as a result.

15 One spy was known as the White Rabbit because he kept disappearing – like the character in Lewis Carroll's *Alice's Adventures in Wonderland*. His real name was Forest Yeo-Thomas. He parachuted into France many times during World War II to organize the resistance against the Germans. He narrowly escaped capture many times, and when he was finally captured, he escaped!

▲ Each letter typed on an Enigma machine became a different letter in the final message. Only someone with another Enigma would know what had really been typed.

The Cold War

▲ Between 1961 and 1991 the German capital city, Berlin, was divided by the Berlin Wall. Spies crossed between Communist East Berlin and free West Berlin.

16 There was lots of spying during the Cold War. From the 1940s to 1991, the US and the Soviet Union (USSR) were enemies. This was partly because the US was against Communism – the political system of the USSR. Each nation used spies to find out about the plans and secret weapons of the other.

17 Some ordinary Americans passed secrets to the USSR. Julius and Ethel Rosenburg seemed like an average American couple, but they were actually spies. They helped pass the secrets of America's atomic bomb to the Russians in the 1940s. When they were found out, it started a wave of fear in America about all communists.

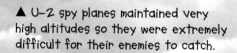

▲ U-2 spy planes maintained very high altitudes so they were extremely difficult for their enemies to catch.

18 In 1956, the US began using a plane called the U-2 to spy on the USSR. The U-2 could fly at such a great height that it was very difficult for the Russians to shoot down, but it could still take good pictures of the Russian military bases.

◄ One of the main aims of Cold War spies was to discover the locations of secret missile sites.

▲ The Russians finally discovered Harvey's Hole when heat from the tunnel melted a clear line of snow on the surface.

19 **Harvey's Hole was a spy tunnel.** During the Cold War, control of the German city of Berlin was divided between the West and the USSR. In 1954, the US dug a tunnel 500 metres in length from their side of Berlin under the Soviet side. From inside the tunnel they could listen in on secret messages. The spy tunnel picked up nearly half a million messages before it was discovered.

20 **In the 1930s the Russians secretly recruited a group of Cambridge University students as spies.** Two of them, Donald Maclean and Guy Burgess, went on to hold important posts in the British government until they were found out and fled to Russia in 1951. Another, Kim Philby, managed to become a senior officer in Britain's spy service MI5 before he too was found out and escaped to Russia in 1963.

QUIZ

1. Who were the two enemies in the Cold War?
2. When did the Cold War end?
3. In which country was the Berlin Wall?

Answers:
1. The USA and Russia 2. 1991 3. Germany

15

Networks and organizations

◀ Far left: During his presidency George Bush had daily briefings from NSC and CIA officials.

Left: The CIA building looks like an ordinary office, but inside some of the world's most secret spying operations go on.

21 The US spy network is the CIA (Central Intelligence Agency). The headquarters are in Langley, Virginia. The National Clandestine Service (NCS) is a top-secret branch of the CIA. NCS agents work to gather foreign intelligence and recruit contacts to give them information, or 'HUMINT' (HUMan INTelligence).

22 Russia's spy network is the FSB – Federal Security Service. During the Cold War, Russia was part of the Soviet Union (USSR). The spy network for the USSR was the KGB. When the USSR broke up in 1991 the KGB became the FSB. The FSB has over half a million agents. They target criminals, drug smugglers, terrorists and the secrets of other countries.

▼ The main FSB building is in Lubyanka Square in Moscow, Russia.

▶ Intelligence agencies are in constant contact with their political leaders. Shown here in February 2008, then Russian president Vladimir Putin (right) speaks to FSB director Nikolay Patrushev

▶ After Mordechai Vanunu revealed Israel's nuclear weapons programme to the world in 1986, he was snatched in Rome by Mossad agents. While in custody Vanunu wrote details of his kidnapping on his hand so watching journalists would know what had happened to him.

23 **Israel's spy network is called Mossad, which is the Israeli word for 'The Institute'.** Mossad has a special secret division called *Metsada*, which means Special Operations. Metsada's task is to undermine Israel's enemies and to attack terrorist bases.

24 **The SIS (Secret Intelligence Services) is the spy network for the United Kingdom.** It is also sometimes known by its old name of MI6 (MI stood for 'Military Intelligence'). SIS agents track terrorists, gather information about people or countries that hold powerful weapons around the world, and also infiltrate international crime rings.

◀ Far left: British agent Lionel 'Buster' Crabb vanished in 1956 while diving to spy on the new propeller on a Soviet warship visiting Southampton.
Left: SIS headquarters in London, UK.

Recruitment and training

The OFFICIAL SECRET INTELLIGENCE SERVICE WEBSITE

Welcome to the official website of the Secret Intelligence Service (SIS).

As Britain's secret service, SIS provides the British Government with a global covert capability to promote and defend the national security and economic well-being of the United Kingdom.

SIS operates world-wide to collect secret foreign intelligence in support of the British Government's policies and objectives.

Regional instability, terrorism, the proliferation of weapons of mass destruction and illegal narcotics are among the major challenges of the 21st century. SIS assists the government to meet these challenges. To do this effectively SIS must protect the secrets of its sources and methods. This factor is reflected in our website.

SIS
SECRET INTELLIGENCE SERVICE

▶ SIS OR MI6?
What's in a name!
Officially we are SIS but many people know us as MI6...

◀ The British SIS advertises job vacancies on its website. To find out more go to www.sis.gov.uk and click on 'Careers'.

25 **Spy networks advertise for new spies!** Employees apply for jobs just like everyone else, and some agencies even sponsor recruits through further education. In wartime many people volunteer out of a sense of duty to their country. Others are only persuaded to spy in return for large sums of money.

26 **The ability to speak a foreign language is useful for spies working abroad.** UK security services look in particular for people who speak Chinese, Arabic or Farsi. Agencies might also look for people with knowledge of international or criminal affairs, or people with mathematical or scientific skills who could analyze intelligence.

◀ Kim Philby was secretly recruited to spy for Russia while at Cambridge University in the 1930s. He then got a job in the British secret service, and was able to pass top-secret information to his Russian bosses.

◄ Computer hacking is a valuable spy skill, so secret services may try to recruit at hacking conventions.

29 **No spy is licensed to kill.** Unlike fictional spy James Bond, no spy is officially allowed to commit murder – not that it never happens. Governments may issue secret orders for their agents to kill, but if an agent is caught, the government will deny all knowledge.

27 **Spies have to be skilful.** A spy's career often starts with a long training course. Some skills, such as learning a foreign language and improving IT skills, can appear perfectly innocent. Others, such as learning to pick locks, hack into computers, break into offices or disable security systems, are much more devious.

I DON'T BELIEVE IT!

The best sources of information are often weak people. Agencies call these people 'MICE', because they are willing to betray their friends or countries because of Money, Ideology (beliefs), Compromise or Ego (selfishness).

28 **Some spies are trained to fight.** Agents may have to undertake potentially dangerous tasks, and might not be authorized to alert anyone if they get into trouble. Survival skills they may need include knowing how to live off the land, use a variety of weapons and speak multiple languages fluently.

► Many spies train in armed combat just like soldiers.

30 **Spies don't usually operate alone.** Field agents (spies who go on missions) work with teams of people to provide back-up and specialist skills. Every mission is managed by a case officer, while handlers pass information between the agent and their employers at the intelligence agency.

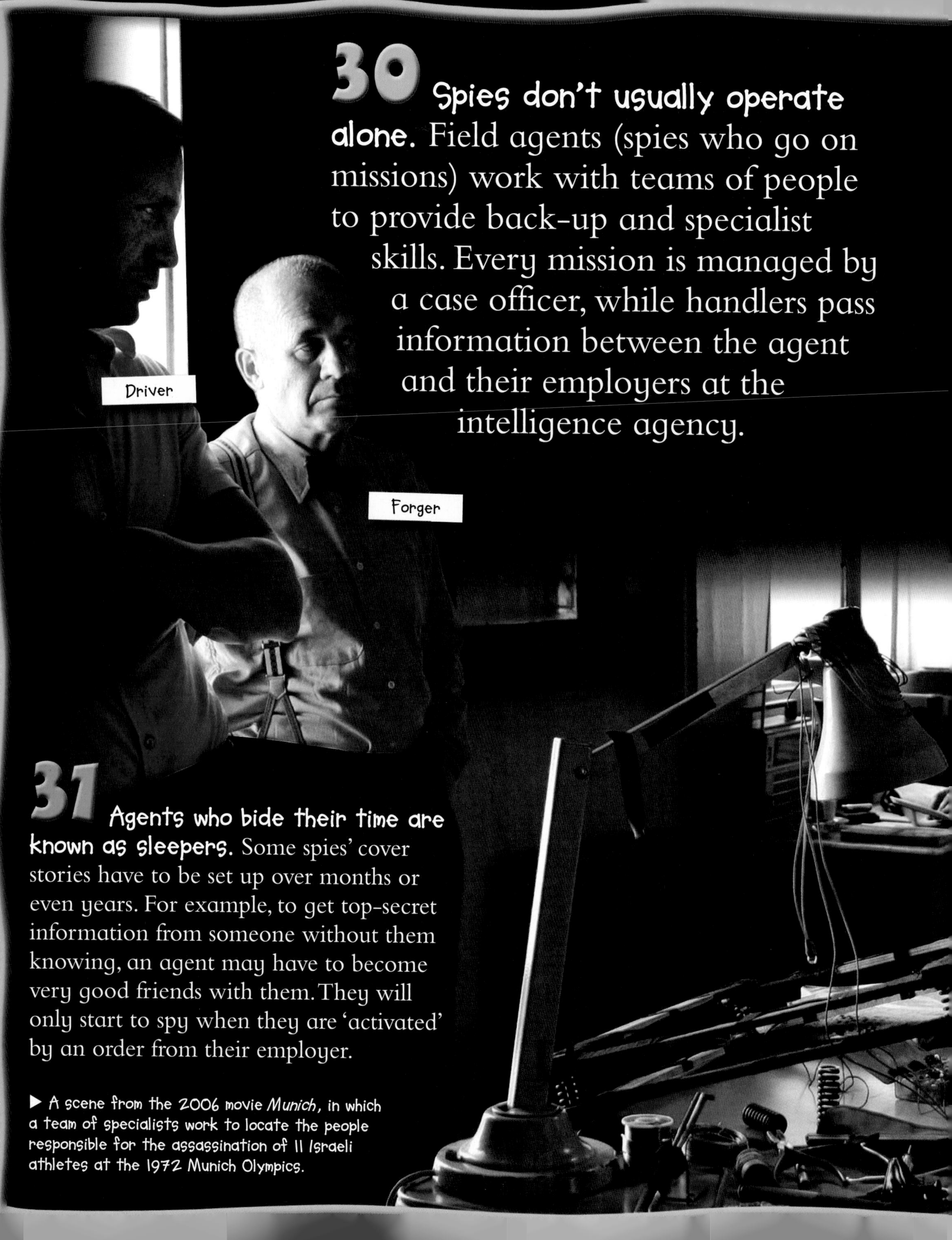

Driver

Forger

31 **Agents who bide their time are known as sleepers.** Some spies' cover stories have to be set up over months or even years. For example, to get top-secret information from someone without them knowing, an agent may have to become very good friends with them. They will only start to spy when they are 'activated' by an order from their employer.

▶ A scene from the 2006 movie *Munich*, in which a team of specialists work to locate the people responsible for the assassination of 11 Israeli athletes at the 1972 Munich Olympics.

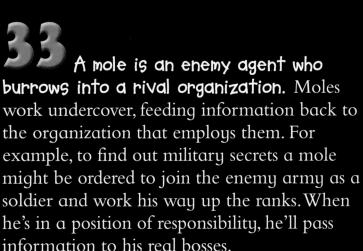

32 **Spy teams have special skills.** An agent may need weapons, a false identity or observation equipment to complete a mission, and these are provided by a technical team. Skilled forgers make false documents and set up ways in which the agent can fool security systems.

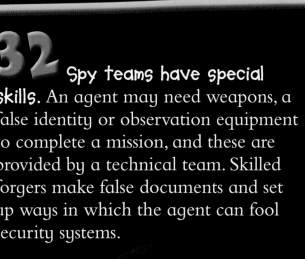

Clean-up

Field agent

Explosives expert

33 **A mole is an enemy agent who burrows into a rival organization.** Moles work undercover, feeding information back to the organization that employs them. For example, to find out military secrets a mole might be ordered to join the enemy army as a soldier and work his way up the ranks. When he's in a position of responsibility, he'll pass information to his real bosses.

34 **Leakers are ordinary people who expose secret information.** For example, if an employee of a company discovers that the company is doing something illegal, they may anonymously 'leak' the information. Features on special websites allow people to leak information while keeping their identity secret.

Leakers may need to gather evidence of their company's wrongdoing when no one is around.

21

Listening in

35 **Spies listen in on conversations using bugs.** A bug is a small microphone with a radio transmitter to carry the sound it picks up. Bugs come in all shapes and sizes and can be hidden under desks, concealed inside pens or even tucked inside a shirt button.

Microphone

Battery

Circuit board

Antenn

Switch

▲ X-rays reveal a microphone and radio transmitter hidden in an ordinary cigarette packet.

36 **A US ambassador's gift was bugged!** In the 1950s, the USSR presented the US ambassador to Moscow with a replica of the US Great Seal. The ambassador hung it in his office, unaware that the seal concealed a bug that enabled the Soviets to listen to his conversations. This bug needed no electrical power and was operated by the vibrations of radio waves alone, so it was very hard to detect.

The bugged eagle seal hung on the wall above the desk of the US ambassador to Moscow.

37 **Even shoes can be bugged.** During 1960s, the US ambassador in Czechoslovakia ordered some shoes from America. The Czech secret service intercepted them, planting a bug inside one heel. Whenever the ambassador wore the shoes, the Czechs could listen in on his conversations.

◄ One way to hear what your target is saying wherever he goes is to hide a bug inside the heel of his shoe!

OUTPUT **LEVEL**

0 1 2 8 12 20 30 45 65 90

0   30   60   90   120   150   180   210   240   270   300   330   36(

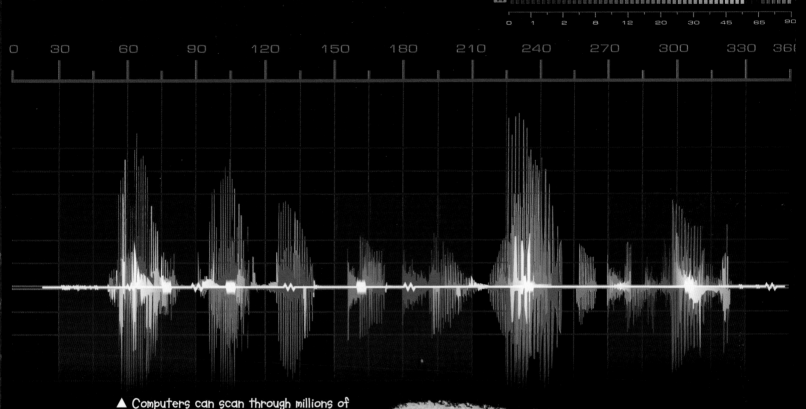

▲ Computers can scan through millions of calls and quickly pick out a target from the unique sound patterns in a person's voice.

38 **Phone or wire-tapping means listening in to phone conversations.** It is quite a simple thing to do – with wireless phones and mobiles, agents use radio receivers that tune into the right signal. Spy networks can also tap into the telephone exchange, so they can monitor any calls without fear of detection.

HOW TO OVERHEAR

You will need:
microphone (mic)   recording device
metal mixing bowl

1. Set up the recorder and mic.
2. Record your friends talking, first standing close to the mic, then further away. At what distance does the mic fail to pick up sound?
3. Now aim the inside of the bowl at your friends, holding the mic in the middle. It should now pick up sounds from much further away.

39 **Making a call could give you away.** GPS (Global Positioning System) receivers inside some phones use satellites to pinpoint the phone's location when you make a call! Spies can also target calls using 'voice recognition'. Computers scan through millions of calls per second, flagging voices that they have been programmed to recognize. This is called data mining.

◄ Thanks to satellite technology, electronic eavesdropping now happens on a global scale.

Keeping watch

▼ CCTV keeps even ordinary people under constant surveillance.

40 **Surveillance is an important part of spying.** Spies can find out vital information about a target, such as where they go and who they meet, by secretly observing them over a period of time. It is important that the person under surveillance does not realize they are being watched. The agent has to stay hidden, watch from a distance or set up technological equipment to watch for them.

41 **CCTV (Closed Circuit Television) is used to spy on the public.** CCTV cameras are perched on buildings all over most modern cities, watching the movements of regular people. In the UK, there are more than five million of these cameras watching the streets. The average Londoner is filmed more than 300 times every day.

42 **Remote surveillance means watching from a distance.** It can be difficult to get close enough to someone to observe them without them noticing, but with the aid of cameras and bugs you can spy from afar. Radio and satellite technology are so advanced that an agent can keep someone under remote surveillance from the other side of the world if necessary.

QUIZ

1. What do the letters CCTV stand for?
2. What does 'remote surveillance' mean?
3. Who invented the Minox spy camera?

Answers:
1. Closed Circuit Television
2. Watching from a distance
3. Walter Zapp

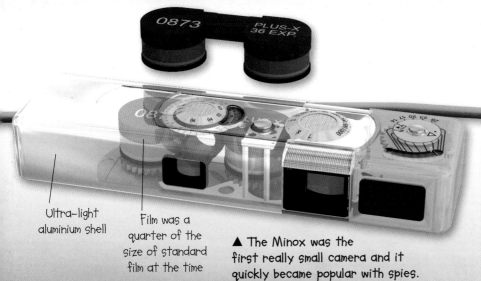

Ultra-light aluminium shell

Film was a quarter of the size of standard film at the time

▲ The Minox was the first really small camera and it quickly became popular with spies.

▶ This tiny video camera is so small it can be easily hidden for secret filming.

43 **The Minox is the most famous spy camera.** In the 1930s, Latvian Walter Zapp invented a small camera that could always be carried. The size of a cigarette lighter, the Minox took high-quality pictures and was soon being used by spies. It was in use until the 1990s.

44 **Video cameras are now so small they can be hidden almost anywhere.** Those with digital video recorders can be smaller than dice, and concealed inside anything from a button to a pen.

45 **Moonpenny is the code name for America's European surveillance post.** The CIA listen in to every phone call and TV signal sent across Europe via satellite using a radio antenna on the ground that picks up all the signals. The antenna is code named 'Moonpenny' and is at Menwith Hill, Yorkshire, England.

▼ The covered satellite dishes or 'radomes' of the Moonpenny surveillance system at Menwith Hill in Yorkshire.

Secrets of concealment

46 Spies have special hiding places, which they call 'concealment devices' or 'diversion safes'. The best way to hide something important such as a classified document or top-secret gadget is to make it look unremarkable, so spies make hiding places inside ordinary things, such as books, pens or even toys.

47 A book is a good concealment device. You can easily hide something flat inside one, or hollow out pages to conceal something bigger. It would take a long time for someone to find the right book in a library, or even a large bookcase.

◀ Everyday objects such as books make good hiding places for spy equipment.

CHAPTER ONE

GETTING THE MESSAGE

You are a spy and your task is to get a secret message to one of your friends, who is a fellow spy. A third friend is the spy-catcher whose task is to intercept the message. Leave the message somewhere secret in your school grounds. Your fellow spy is not allowed to pick it up until the next day. The spy-catcher has to find the message, or catch you or your fellow spy dropping it off or picking it up.

◄ New T-ray scanners can see right through clothes to reveal hidden weapons – perfect for catching both spies and terrorists.

Russia claimed British agents were using the fake rock to deliver and retrieve data within Russia.

48 In 2006, Britain was accused of spying in Russia using a fake rock. Russian pictures showed British agents picking up a rock in a Moscow park. Inside the rock was a radio transmitter, which Russia claimed the British were using to send information. It caused a scandal because the British were supposed to have stopped spying in Russia in 1994.

49 A harmless object can conceal a deadly weapon. If an agent carries a weapon he may need to get it past security guards and scanners. To do this he has to disguise it as something else – ideally something small that no one would guess was dangerous. Spies have even been known to conceal pistols inside tubes of lipstick.

50 A dead drop is a secret location where agents leave information for someone else to pick up. The location must be concealed, such as a hole in a tree or a loose brick in a wall. Once the message has been left, the spy leaves a signal to indicate the information is there. The signal could be anything from a flower in a window to chewing gum on a street sign.

▲ A dead drop spike is an airtight, watertight tube for hiding messages in the ground.

27

Disguises and covers

Hair length and colour are easy things to change

51 A disguise is essential for some spy work. When keeping someone under surveillance, a spy may have to keep changing his appearance, or his target may recognize him and become suspicious. A spy may also need to wear a disguise to keep his identity secret when meeting a contact.

Long wig disguises real hair colour and face shape

False beard

Dark glasses hide eye colour and shape

52 Lawrence of Arabia was famous for his disguise as an Arab. During World War I, British soldier T E Lawrence often put on an Arab headdress and darkened his face for missions in the Middle East to spy on the Turks. He later led the Arabs in revolt against their Turkish rulers and became famous as 'Lawrence of Arabia'.

▲ Disguises have to fit the situation and back up the cover story and an agent may sometimes have to make a quick change.

▶ Baggy, casual clothes are suitable for outdoor surveillance and can hide an agent's build.

Loose clothing can conceal weapons or equipment

53 Small things such as the way you walk can give away your identity. You can make your face look different by applying make-up and changing your hair, but everyone has their own way of walking, and an enemy might be able to identify you from this alone. Spies sometimes put a false heel in one of their shoes to change their walk and avoid detection.

Contact lenses can be worn instead of glasses

◄ It would be impossible for an agent to enter a business or organization dressed in office wear without someone asking who they were, so they would need to have a cover story ready.

54 **Disguises can be permanent.** A temporary disguise is enough for most missions, but if a spy's cover is blown he may need to change his appearance forever. With plastic surgery, you can change someone's face so completely that they become unrecognizable.

GO UNDERCOVER

Try and make a disguise good enough to fool your mum. Wear different clothes, perhaps padded out to make you look fatter. Wear glasses and a hat or a wig to cover your hair. Practise a different voice and walk – but don't overdo it. When you're ready, go outside and ring your doorbell. When your mum comes to the door, pretend that you are one of your friends come to ask you out to play. See if you can fool her for one minute.

Make-up can change skin tone and alter features

Latex 'fattening' alters face shape

High heels can change posture and gait (walk)

► Disguised as a cleaner, an agent can gain access to lots of different areas when fewer people are around. Props such as mops can conceal surveillance equipment.

Padded suit disguises build

55 **The greatest master of disguise was the legendary Chevalier d'Eon.** The Chevalier spied for the French King Louis XV in the 18th century, and could fool anyone with his brilliant disguises. He posed as a beautiful young girl called Genevieve to get important secrets out of the Russian empress, Elizabeth.

Hidden messages

56 **The science of sending hidden messages is called steganography.** It was invented in ancient Greece. Around 500 BC, King Demeratus of Sparta wanted to warn the Greeks that Persia was planning to attack them. He sent a harmless-looking letter to the Greeks, scratched in candle wax on a board, but he had actually written the warning on the board under the wax. The Greeks just had to melt the wax to read it.

57 **A good secret message looks like something else.** Sending what looks like a blank piece of paper to someone is a bit of a giveaway – enemies will guess the paper holds an invisible message. The best way to keep your message secret is to write something ordinary on the paper on top of your invisible message. This is called the cover text.

▶ Secret messages are not always written on paper. In World War I (1914–1918), a message was written on the back of a Belgian female spy in invisible ink, but her captors discovered the message and she was executed.

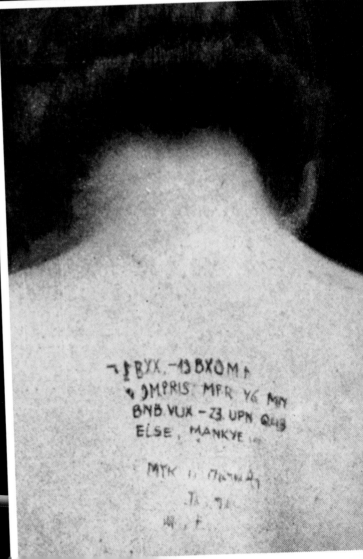

Dear Jo,

I am having a lovely t
Received your message
The locals are all very friendly
Please alert Davis in sur
weather has been really lovely
possible counter—attack
with only a little rain so far.
in early hours of 7.9 —
Please write soon and tell me all

Your friend,

Simon

58

Spies can write secret messages using invisible ink. The right person can make the message visible with the right treatment. Some inks are made visible by heating, some by applying chemicals, while others need to be seen under ultraviolet light.

59

A microdot is a message so small it can only be seen with a special viewer. Spies can take a photograph of a piece of evidence or information such as a message or plans, and reduce the picture so much that it can only be seen under a special magnifying viewer. Microdots are so tiny that they can be hidden in secret chambers inside coins or rings...

The special cameras used to create microdots can reduce a whole paragraph of text to around the size of a full stop at the end of a sentence.

◄ The cover text (in black) of this agent's letter just looks like regular correspondence. The secret message is only revealed under heat from the torch.

British spy Lord Baden Powell pretended to be a butterfly collector, disguising his drawings of enemy military bases (shown in red) in sketches of butterfly wings.

60

Terrorists may send secret messages over the Internet. The Internet uses an electronic code, and messages can be incorporated into this code. Some people believe that the terrorist group al-Qaeda spread messages over the Internet inside harmless-looking pictures. However this is unlikely because the messages could easily be discovered by the powerful computers of the security services.

SEND A SECRET

You will need:
lemon juice   paintbrush   paper

Prepare your secret message. When you're ready, carefully 'write' your message on the paper in lemon juice using a fine paintbrush. All you'll see when you write is a faint damp line and when it dries, it will vanish completely. The receiver just needs to hold the paper up to a heat source such as a lightbulb for the message to appear.

Codes and ciphers

61 Simple messages can be kept secret by putting them in a code that only the right people understand. Using a code means using special symbols, words and letters to disguise your meaning. For example, you might use the code word 'monster' whenever you talk about a horrible aunt secretly to your friends. Armies and police often use code words.

62 The ancient Greeks used a simple method to make codes called a skytale. This was a strip of leather rolled around a rod in a spiral. The strip had a series of letters written on it. When the strip was unrolled, the letters made no sense. But when the strip was wrapped around a rod of the same diameter, they fell into line to spell out the message.

Skytale message

63 Complicated messages can be kept secret using a cipher. A cipher is a system where you swap letters in your original message for different letters, symbols and numbers. For example, substituting the letter A for B, C for D, and so on.

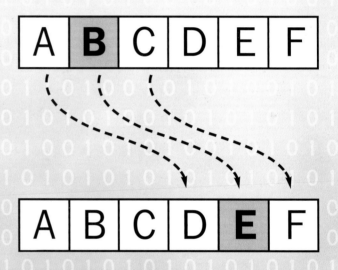

▲ To create a code, Caesar wrote out the alphabet, then wrote it a second time, below the first, with the letters shifted to the right. Using the example above, the message 'Meet at dawn' would become 'Jbbq xq axtk'.

64 The Roman general Julius Caesar invented his own cipher. Caesar sent secret messages to his troops using a cipher he invented called the Caesar Shift. He simply replaced each letter in the message with another letter a few places on in the alphabet. He varied the number of places to keep the secret hidden.

► US Marine 'wind-talkers' send messages in the Navajo language during the war in the Pacific in World War II.

65 In World War II (1939–1945), the language of the Navajo Native Americans gave the US navy an unbreakable spoken code. People would write messages in English, and then the Navajo would speak the message out letter by letter over the radio, using a different Navajo word for each letter. It was impossible for anyone else but a Navajo code-talker to work out the message. The Navajos thought talking over the radio was like sending messages on the wind, so they were known as 'wind-talkers'.

66 One way to break a code is to analyze how often particular letters occur. In any message, letters like 'e' occur frequently, while letters like 'x' are rare. So you can often work what the different symbols in the code mean by analyzing how frequently they occur in the message.

◄ To launch a nuclear attack, the US president has to send out a signal in special codes known as Gold Codes. These are stored in a bag called 'the football', which is carried by a military officer who goes everywhere with the president.

INVENT A CIPHER

Use your own Caesar Shift to make a cipher. Write a message, then re-write it moving every letter a certain number of places on in the alphabet. You could also try making up a symbol for each letter of the alphabet to make it even harder. Make sure you tell the person you want to read the message the rules for how to crack your code – but not in the same letter, because if someone intercepts it then your message won't stay secret for long!

Death and danger

There are many ways to assassinate someone, and some use very harmless-looking items.

67 Film star Lesley Howard was shot down in a plane full of spies during World War II (1939–1945). Howard was flying in the airliner *Ibis* in 1943 when it was attacked by German fighter planes. The *Ibis* was a civilian plane, so why did the Germans want to shoot it down? Later research suggests the real target was Howard, who was actually a spy, and that other spies were on board too.

Trigger

68 Former Russian spy Oleg Gordievsky claims many enemies of Russia are assassinated. Gordievsky believes that Russian agents routinely kill people outside of Russia. In 2006, the Russian parliament passed a law allowing the assassination of enemies of Russia living abroad. During 2007, Gordievsky fell ill. He believed he was poisoned by sleeping pills supplied by Russian spies.

▶ The umbrella that killed Markov contained a gas cylinder that fired poison when the trigger was pushed.

69 An umbrella became a deadly weapon. Bulgarian writer Georgi Markov was an outspoken critic of Bulgaria's leaders. Then in 1978 he was stabbed in the leg with an umbrella while he waited for a London bus. The umbrella was specially designed to inject poison through the tip, and Markov died four days later. It is likely that the man who did it was a Bulgarian spy.

Gas cylinder

70 **The British commander-in-chief Lord Kitchener may have been killed by a spy.** Fritz Duquesne was a South African whose family farm was destroyed by the British, led by Kitchener, in the Boer War in 1902. Determined to have revenge, Duquesne became a spy for Germany in World War I. Posing as a Russian duke, Duquesne gained entry to a ship carrying Kitchener from Scotland to Russia, and then used a radio to guide a German submarine to his position. Duquesne escaped on a raft just before the attack, and Kitchener was killed.

71 **Spies sometimes have to take their own lives.** If an agent is caught he may find it difficult not to give away secrets under torture. On dangerous missions agents may carry suicide pills to take if they are captured. These pills contain fast-acting poisons, which kill the spy quickly before he can give away any information.

◄ Real spies rarely get into situations as hairy as this, but they have to be trained to deal with them. In this scene from *Mission Impossible III* (2003), agent Ethan Hunt (played by Tom Cruise) is ambushed by mercenaries (hired soldiers).

Weapons and gadgets

▲ A gun with a silencer, nicknamed 'the whispering death', is standard equipment for spies.

I DON'T BELIEVE IT!

US scientists are working on creating shark spies. They will implant electrodes in sharks' brains so that they can control them remotely. The sharks could then be used to track vessels through the sea.

72 **The noise of a gunshot attracts attention.** The sound is made mainly by explosive gases escaping very fast – like a balloon popping. Spies often fit their guns with metal tubes called silencers that slow down the release of the gases. They also fire slower, quieter bullets that are just as effective at short range.

73 **The Stinger is a gun disguised as a tube of toothpaste.** It was developed by the CIA for their spies in the Cold War. British spies used guns disguised as cigarettes. The KGB gave their female agents guns disguised as tubes of lipstick that they simply twisted to fire.

▼ A spy or terrorist can be assassinated from a place of safety far away using a powerful telescopic sight.

◄ The ultimate spy gadget is the Aston Martin car used by the fictional spy James Bond in films such as *Die Another Day* (2002).

74
A spy's luggage may not be quite what it seems. In the past, spies often carried long-range radios disguised as ordinary suitcases. Suitcases might also contain special concealed compartments to hide essential equipment from anyone who might open the case. However, modern scanners can show up such secret compartments. Today, spies have to use different methods of concealment. Equipment might be disguised as something harmless to fool the scanners.

75
'Thermal imaging' allows spies to shoot in pitch darkness. Heat creates infrared light, which is invisible to the eye but can be detected and displayed by thermal imaging devices. Human bodies give out heat that thermal-imaging devices detect. Using a gun equipped with a thermal imager, a spy can clearly see his target under the cover of total darkness.

▶ It may be pitch dark, but with thermal imaging your target shows up clearly. Different colours represent different temperatures, from red (hot) to blue (cold).

76
Submarines allow spies to sneak up on enemies underwater. Deep water provides very good cover for spying. During the Cold War, the Americans sent spy submarines into the icy Arctic waters north of Russia. On the seabed they could tap into Russian undersea cables carrying secret messages. They listened in for over 20 years like this without ever being found out. This operation was codenamed 'Ivy Bells'.

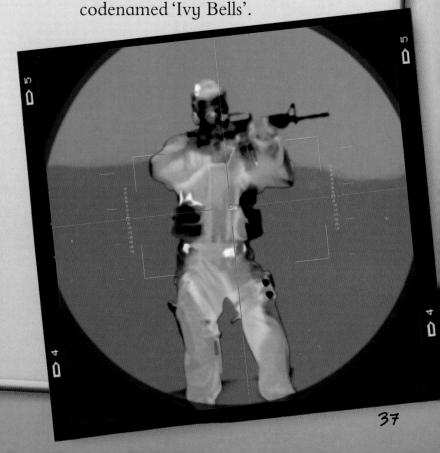

From the air

77 During the American Civil War (1861–1865), Thaddeus Lowe spied in a balloon. Lowe was a balloonist who took people for rides in his balloon at country fairs. When war broke out, Lowe used his balloon to spy on the Confederate army. From the balloon, he could see enemy troops for 40 kilometres around. He reported on what he saw to the Union below through a telegraph cable.

▲ One of the first airborne spies, Thaddeus Lowe spied for the Union from a hydrogen balloon in the US Civil War. Here he prepares for a mission at the Battle of Fair Oaks, Virginia, on 1 June 1862.

78 When Paris was attacked by the Prussians in 1870, the people of Paris used balloons to get secret messages out. People trapped inside the city made balloons to carry out messages and microfilms. The balloons flew only at night so the Prussians would not see them. Despite the dangers, of the 66 balloons that left Paris, 58 arrived safely.

I DON'T BELIEVE IT!

The German airships of World War I were very big, so if they flew low they were easy to shoot down. Spies would dangle on wires in special 'spy baskets' up to 1000 metres below the airship. This allowed the airship to stay high, out of range of enemy guns.

► Aerial reconnaissance in World War II meant flying dangerous missions over enemy territory to take pictures.

79 The first spy planes were used in World War I (1914–1918).

The first successful flight was by the Wright brothers in 1903. Just 12 years later, in World War I, armies realized planes could be used to spy on enemies without sending spies in on the ground. World War I planes had open cockpits, so spy plane pilots held spies by their belts as they leaned out to take pictures of the ground below.

◄ The Lockheed SR-71 'Blackbird' was one of the first 'stealth' planes, with a shape designed to conceal the plane from radar detection.

80 Modern spy planes use special technology to avoid detection.

Usually, planes can be detected by radar, which works by detecting radio waves that bounce off planes. Stealth planes use a range of techniques to make them invisible to radar. They are coated in special paint that soaks up radar waves, and they are specially shaped so that the radar waves don't bounce off them in the usual way.

81 Photos taken from the air in 2003 appeared to show that Iraq had dangerous weapons.

In 2002, the US claimed that Iraq had Weapons of Mass Destruction (WMD), which use chemicals to kill lots of people at once. Pictures taken from the air seemed to support this, so the US invaded Iraq. No weapons were ever found, and it is uncertain as to whether they were moved or destroyed, or if the photos were misleading.

Watching the world

82 **Satellites in space are a vital part of international spying.** Spy satellites keep track of armies, pick up signals from agents' radio transmitters, send secret coded messages and monitor terrorist activity.

▼ In 2003, Japan launched its first pair of spy satellites aboard the H-2A rocket to keep watch on neighbouring North Korea.

83 **US spy satellites are controlled by the ELINT system.** ELINT stands for ELectronic INTelligence, and the system is run by a secret organization called the NGA (National Geospatial-Intelligence Agency).

Modern powerful satellites may be able to read car number plates from space.

84 **The latest US Ikon Keyhole spy satellites can photograph things that are just a few centimetres across.** Some may have cameras that can read a book cover. Spy satellites will soon be able to track the movement of something as small as a mouse from space.

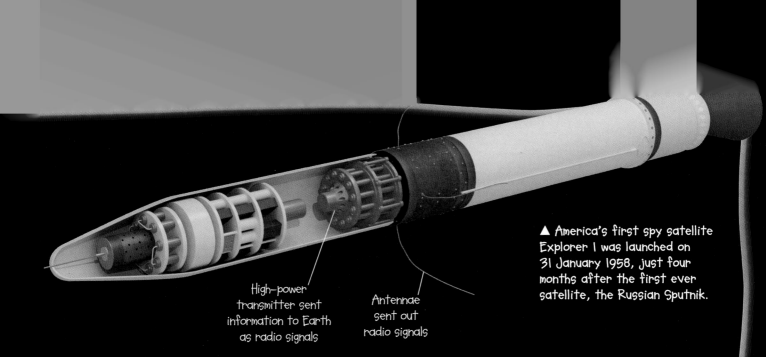

High-power transmitter sent information to Earth as radio signals

Antennae sent out radio signals

▲ America's first spy satellite Explorer I was launched on 31 January 1958, just four months after the first ever satellite, the Russian Sputnik.

85

The three US Parcae satellites can track the position, speed and direction of any ship, anywhere. They pick up signals that ships put out such as navigation and radio signals, and pinpoint locations so accurately that ships can be targeted by missiles fired on the other side of the world.

86

Some satellites are built to detect heat. They have detectors called thermal imagers, which can detect someone hiding inside a hut or heat from a camouflaged target or underground bunker. They can also detect the hot exhaust from a nuclear missile within seconds of its launch.

87

Some spy satellites are mistaken for alien spacecraft. The US government denied the existence of their first surveillance satellites, so many people thought they were UFOs (Unidentified Flying Objects). The three Parcae satellites were particularly mysterious, because they flew in a triangle, which convinced people they must be UFOs.

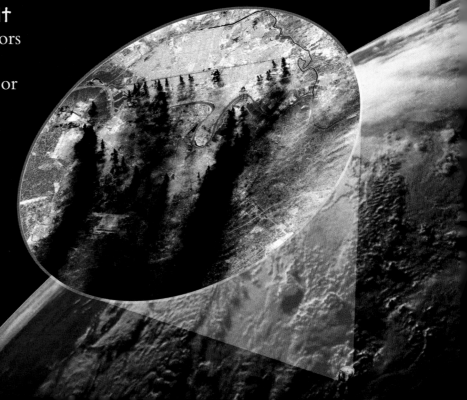

► Satellites with thermal imaging equipment reveal activity on the ground. Here, black smoke plumes from the burning of oil are visible around the city of Baghdad in Iraq.

Hacking in

88 **Computers connected to the Internet can be spied on by hackers.** Computers use codes and passwords to stop the wrong people connecting to them, but hackers can often find a way to get past this protection to gain access to secret information.

89 **Sometimes hackers can gain control of your computer.** If a hacker installs a keylogging programme it will log every key you hit on the keyboard – including your secret passwords. There is also a type of programme called a Trojan horse that appears to perform positive functions but actually takes over your computer completely.

▲ British music student Richard Pryce, known as Datastream Cowboy, hacked into American Air Force computers as a prank.

▶ Gary McKinnon, known as Solo, trespassed on networks owned by NASA, the US Army, Navy, Air Force, and Department of Defense.

90 **Hackers have special software programmes to help them.** People often make it easy for hackers by using obvious things such as their name for a password. In case they don't, hackers have special password-cracking software to help them find more difficult passwords. The software runs through combinations of letters and numbers very, very fast until it hits the right one.

91 **Hackers enjoy the challenge of hacking into secret computers.** In 2002, a hacker who called himself Solo hacked into US military computers from his bedroom in London. Solo's real name was Gary McKinnon, and he claimed he was looking for evidence that UFOs were real. Two other British teenagers, Richard Pryce and Matthew Bevan, hacked into US military computers for fun in 1994.

◀ Computer experts fight a constant battle to prevent hackers and other mischief-makers interfering with the world's computer networks. Here, experts at the LAC (Little eArth Corporation – an Internet security firm in Japan) monitor a 'cyber attack' as it happens.

How to catch a spy

92 Spies can make mistakes.
Undercover agents work hard to build strong fake identities, but it's not impossible to catch them out. Spy-catchers may hide cameras and microphones on themselves when going to meet a suspected spy, so that if the spy makes a mistake and says the wrong thing, they'll get a record of the slip that gives them away.

▲ Iris scanners analyze features in the coloured tissue around the pupil. Every iris pattern is unique, so the scanners are incredibly hard to fool.

93 Biometric identity tests can foil spies.
Skilled forgers can make false passports, and trained researchers can work out secret passwords, but it's not so easy to fake your body. Biometric tests identify someone using parts of their anatomy such as the fingertips or the iris of the eye. These things are unique to each of us and are very hard to fake. Special scanners can now perform biometric tests instantly. Many computers have fingerprint scanners to stop the wrong people using them.

▶ An electronic fingerprint scan can provide instant identification and block entry to any intruders.

An enemy spy is cornered after a successful sting operation.

95 A trap to catch a spy or a criminal is called a sting. One way is to offer the spy or a criminal what seems to be a golden opportunity. For example, you might pretend to know a secret way into a place the spy wants to get into. Then all you have to do is arrange for secret cameras and microphones to be in place to catch him giving himself away.

94 Facial scanners can identify someone without them knowing. They can scan crowds, using special cameras to take pictures of a face from several angles at once. The pictures provide a complete set of measurements of the shape of the face. The scanner can then identify a face from its measurements and tell you if it belongs to an intruder.

▼ A face recognition scanner can spot anyone on its 'wanted' database instantly – sometimes even through a disguise.

96 The most famous spy is fictional!

British writer Ian Fleming created James Bond in 1953. Bond (code name 007) works for the British secret service and is always suave and charming, even in dangerous situations. Fleming wrote 12 Bond novels and there have been 22 movies. Charlie Higson's *Young Bond* books show Bond as a teenager.

▼ James Bond often finds himself in highly dangerous situations. In the 2008 movie *Quantum of Solace*, in which Bond is played by Daniel Craig, he has to stop an evil villain taking control of a country's valuable resource.

QUIZ

1. What was James Bond's code name?
2. What was Percy Blakeney's secret identity?
3. What is Jason Bourne's real name?

Answers:
1. 007
2. The Scarlet Pimpernel
3. David Webb

97 Jason Bourne is the American spy with a mysterious past.

In the films based on Robert Ludlum's books, Bourne is not his real name. His real name is David Webb – and Bourne is the name of a double agent that Webb kills. But even Bourne doesn't know who he really he is.

98 The *Spykids* films are about child spies. The first film starred Alexa Vega and Daryl Sabara as Carmen and Juni Cortez. They are the children of two spies who were once on opposite sides but fell in love.

▲ In the *Spykids* films, teenage spies Carmen and Juni Cortez employ all kinds of gadgets in their fight against evil.

99 Alex Ryder is the teenage spy in films based on the series of books by Anthony Horowitz. The stories begin when 14-year-old orphan Alex investigates the mysterious death of his uncle. He soon discovers that his uncle was a spy. The British secret service take Alex on and send him on dangerous missions.

▶ Like James Bond, Alex Ryder has to escape from potentially deadly situations, such as this one in the 2006 movie *Stormbreaker*.

100 Appearances can be misleading. The Scarlet Pimpernel is the hero of a play and book written by Baroness Orczy in 1903. Set in the French Revolution in the 1790s, Percy Blakeney is a seemingly silly English lord whose alter-ego the Scarlet Pimpernel is a brilliant spy who goes to France to rescue those in danger during the Revolution.

Index

Entries in **bold** refer to main subject entries. Entries in *italics* refer to illustrations.